Published by Peaceful Light Publishing

Hardcover ISBN: 9781662902475,
eISBN: 9781662902482

This book is printed on acid free paper.
Printed in the United States of America

PEACEFUL LIGHT
Body Core Wisdom For Youthful Hearts

ANDREW SHUGYO DAIJO BONNICI, PH.D.
Master Zen Teacher, Trainer, And Counselor
Doctor Of Humanistic Depth Psychology

DEDICATION

This book is dedicated to my Mom and Dad, my lifelong lover and soulmate Diana, my two loving sons Tony and Eric, my daughter-in-heart Amber-san, and my four precious grandchildren Meira, Sage, Portia, and Bodhi.

CARTOON ILLUSTRATION

All the cartoon illustrations in this book are used to visually support and transmit the body core teachings of *Peaceful Light*. I bow with gratitude to the artists who created and graciously shared these cartoon images for use in this book. Most of the cartoon illustrations are royalty-free licensed images that I purchased from *Dreamtime.Com* and *Vectortoons.Com*. A few of the cartoon illustrations are freely-licensed public domain images acquired from *Pixabay.Com* and *Wikimedia Commons*.

By slightly modifying one of the cartoon illustrations from *Wikimedia Commons,* I was able to create a cartoon image of myself that appears on the front cover. I also modified all the cartoon characters by creating a *shining rainbow light* at the center of their bodies. I hope you enjoy all the cartoon images as much as I enjoyed finding their true place in this book.

• CONTENTS •

About This Book

I wrote *Peaceful Light* just for you if you are a curious child, a truth-seeking teenager, or a grown-up of any age who embodies the curiosity and wonder of beginner's heartmind.

Peaceful Light introduces you to an inner glowing stillness that exists at the center of your body and the bodies of all human beings.

Peaceful Light reveals how your inner glowing stillness connects you to the Great Smartness of Mother Nature and the Infinite Universe as a Whole.

Peaceful Light explains how your inner glowing stillness has always been your true-Self from the moment you were born.

Peaceful Light will teach you how to joyfully live from the glowing stillness of your true-Self while expressing love and deep caring for yourself, your family, your friends, and all the beings and things you meet in your everyday life.

As you start reading, studying, and practicing the body core wisdom in *Peaceful Light,* I encourage you to openly share your surprising experiences and your growing understanding with everyone who loves you.

With Blessings,

Dr. Bonnici

Enjoy Your Journey Into
The Great Smartness Of
Your Peaceful Light.

Imagine All People Sharing
The World As One Family

Imagine All Religions
Guided By A Peaceful Light

How To Be Who You Truly Are

Sitting quietly alone, feel your body with all its bones. Not thinking about this or that, just be alert like a Siamese cat. Breathing only through your nose, loosen any tightness in your clothes. Enjoy each breath like a gentle breeze, and simply smile without a sneeze. Follow each breath into your body core, and feel the warm still glow that is silently sure.

As the warm still glow rises to your heart and mind, your peaceful light will begin to shine. Shining here, shining there, you will be completely aware. Aware of love, aware of light, you will be humbly noble and upright. Knowing who you truly are, you will go very far. Very far and very near, your greatness will not be stopped by fear. Becoming all you can become, you will shine like the brilliant sun.

Shugyō

The Soft Whisper Of Your Core-Self

Precious One, I have a secret to tell you. It is a very special secret about a soft still whisper that happens at the center of your body. This soft still whisper at the center of your body is really the great smartness of your *core-Self.* We call it *core-Self* because it softly whispers at the core center of our whole body.

Precious One, your core-Self is the true-Self that softly whispers to all human beings from the core center of their bodies. This is why we call our core-Self, *the true-Self of all human beings.*

Precious One, when your heart feels the soft still whisper of your core-Self, you will overflow with love for yourself, your family, your friends, and all human beings. When your brain feels the soft still whisper of your core-Self, your fearful thoughts will melt away, your worries will vanish, and your stressed mind will be at peace.

Precious One, this is why your core-Self is an endless treasure inside your body. The soft whisper of your core-Self is really a stillness that knows without thinking or figuring. This soft whisper is always still whether you are thinking, feeling, resting, playing, or running. Your core-Self sees into the future without looking ahead. It listens to the whole universe without ears. It guides your heart to accept all beings and things just as they are. When you know your core-Self just like this, you will realize that you have been a great smartness and a still brilliance from the time you were born.

Great Smartness Shines
Like The Rainbow From The
Center Of Your Whole Body.

Feeling The Soft Whisper In Your Body

Precious One, your core-Self does not whisper from the heart inside your chest or the brain inside your head. It does not whisper from your ears; it does not whisper from your passing thoughts or feelings. Your core-Self softly whispers from the true center of your whole body. This is very important to understand!

Precious One, the best way to feel the still whisper of core-Self is to find a quiet place where you can be alone. When you find a quiet place to sit down, gently put your lips together and begin to breathe through your nose. As you breathe in through your nose, fill your belly with air like a balloon. Don't push your belly out. Just let it fill up by itself. As your belly fills with air, you will feel a warm still glow just two inches below your belly button. This warm still glow that you feel at the true center of your whole body is your core-Self.

Precious One, when you breathe in and feel the warm still glow of your core-Self, don't hold your breath. Simply let the air flow slowly out through your nose all by itself. It is important not to push your air out. As you keep on breathing in and out just like this, you will feel totally awake to the warm still glow of your core-Self that happens at the center of your whole body.

Precious One, if you start paying attention to the passing thoughts inside your brain or the feelings they arouse, you will forget to breathe into your body core center. Then you will fall asleep in your heady thinking, get lost in your passing feelings, and loose touch with the warm still glow of your core-Self.

Precious One, if this happens to you, do not judge yourself. It is normal to sometimes fall asleep in your passing thoughts and the feelings they arouse. When you realize that you fell asleep in your heady thinking, celebrate your awakened knowing and gently start breathing again into your body core center. As you do just this, you will begin to feel the warm still glow of your core-Self that has never left you even though you were asleep in your passing thoughts and feelings.

A Frog Sits Quietly Alone,
Smiling With Each Breath,
Just Loving His Simple Life.

The Still Peaceful Light Of Core-Self

Precious One, the warm still glow of your core-Self is really a great smartness that softly whispers at the center of your whole body. The great smartness of your core-Self softly whispers without speaking. This means that the soft whisper of core-Self cannot be heard with your ears. The great smartness of core-Self softly whispers without words, sounds, or letters. It does not shout or yell. It does not judge or blame. It softly speaks with a warm glowing stillness just two inches below your belly button. This is why we call core-Self *the great smartness of a peaceful light that remains perfectly still at the center of our whole body.*

Precious One, the peaceful light of your core-Self shines with a still calmness and a brilliant knowing that you can completely trust in your everyday life. As you trust the still calmness and brilliant knowing of your peaceful light, it will always guide you to live with honesty, courage, kindness, confidence, and humility.

Precious One, as you live from the *peaceful light* of your core-Self, you will feel a deep trust in each passing moment, a deep trust in the great smartness of your body, a deep trust in your basic goodness, a deep trust in mother nature, and a deep trust in the universe as a whole.

Precious One, when you live in complete trust just like this, you will think with an open and curious mind. You will take care of yourself and others with a loving and tender heart. Then you will know with your whole body that you are living a caring, trusting, and loving life for the peace and happiness of all human beings.

A Grasshopper Winks
As He Feels The Glowing
Peace At His Body Center.

Everyone Is Born With Their Peaceful Light

Precious One, your core-Self has been softly whispering about the great smartness of your peaceful light from the day you were born. Always remember that this soft whisper happens inside the body of every human being from the moment of their birth.

Precious One, our core-Self continues to softly whisper inside our bodies as we grow from being a baby, a young child, a teenager, an adult, and an elderly person. It does not matter if we think about core-Self or not. It does not matter if we believe in core-Self or not. The great smartness of core-Self softly whispers to all human beings from the time they are born without ever stopping. This soft whisper of core-Self encourages all of us to trust the guidance of our peaceful light as we daily practice living, loving, and learning together.

Precious One, always remember that core-Self softly whispers inside the body of every human being from the time they are born until the time they die. It does not matter where they came from or the color of their skin. It does not matter how much or how little they know inside their brain. It does not matter if they are rich or poor. It does not matter whether they are sick or healthy. It does not matter if they believe in a God or not. No matter what our age or what we believe in, the soft whisper of core-Self is always calling us to be a peaceful light for ourselves, our loved ones, our friends, everyone we meet, and the world as a whole.

A Panda Simply Enjoys His Peaceful Light While Resting On An Old Tree Branch.

Why We Cannot Own Our Peaceful Light

Precious One, from the moment of your birth, core-Self keeps softly whispering an awesome mystery to your whole body. While you are alive, your core-Self softly whispers that the great smartness of your peaceful light is not just happening inside your body and the bodies of all human beings. Your core-Self keeps daily whispering that the great smartness of your peaceful light, happening at the center of your whole body, is also happening at the center of all beings and things throughout the whole universe. This includes everything from the very smallest, like atoms, cells, and molecules, to the very largest like planets, stars, and galaxies.

Precious One, I know how hard it is to understand this awesome mystery with your thinking brain. The only way to understand the mystery softly whispered by your core-Self is with your whole body.

All you have to do is sit quietly alone, breathe into your center, and feel the warm still glow of your core-Self. When you feel the warm still glow of your core-Self, you will know with your whole body that you share the great smartness of a peaceful light with all beings and things throughout the infinite universe.

Precious One, this is why we cannot own the great smartness of a peaceful light that happens at the center of our body. This is why the peaceful light of core-Self does not belong to you or me. We cannot own the great smartness of our peaceful light like we own objects or things in our life. The great smartness of our peaceful light really belongs to the whole universe.

Precious One, when your whole body understands the awesome mystery of core-Self just like this, you will daily shine your peaceful light on all beings and things just as they are. Then you will always take good care of them without trying to own them, control them, or dominate them.

The Great Smartness Of the
Whole Universe Is At The Center
Of All Beings And Things.

You Are The Peaceful Moment Of Now

Precious One, the great smartness of your core-Self is a still flashing moment of peaceful light that happens at the center of your body and the universe as a whole. This means that the still flashing moment of peaceful light that you feel inside your body is also happening all at once at the center of all beings and things. A still flashing moment of peaceful light that happens all at once at the center of all beings and things cannot be understood in the passage of clock time as we know it. This is why we call each flashing moment of peaceful light, *'The timeless moment of Now.'*

Precious One, *the timeless moment of Now is really the* great smartness of a peaceful light that happens as core-Self inside your body while being everywhere all at once. This *timeless moment of Now* that is the peaceful light of the whole universe is who you really are.

11

Precious One, although we can measure the passage of clock time as we know it, we cannot measure *the timeless moment of Now* that happens everywhere all at once. The passage of clock time that people know is really a painting of time that was created by their thinking brain. This painting of time includes seconds, minutes, hours, days and years. When we see things through the painting of time inside our brain, everything goes from the past, to the present, and into the future. This painting of time is very important in our everyday lives. It helps us know when it is time to wake up, when it is time for work or school, when it is time to play, and when it is time to go home.

Precious One, as you live in the daily passage of time with others, I encourage you to follow clock time while feeling the peaceful light of your core-Self. When you use clock time while feeling the peaceful light of your core-Self, you will always enjoy being the *timeless moment of Now* wherever you go and whatever you do. Then you will happily use clock time with ease in your body, peace in your heart, and wonder in your mind.

He Sits In Peace! Just Being
The Timeless Moment Of Now
With The Whole Universe.

You Are Not Alone In The Peaceful Light

Precious One, always remember that your peaceful light is *the timeless moment of Now* that shines inside your body while being everywhere all at once. As the *peaceful light at the center of* your body is the same peaceful light that happens at the center of all beings and things, all beings and things are your true friends in *the peaceful light of Now.* This is why you can feel a close, caring, and respectful relationship with all beings and things that meet your core-Self in everyday life. This includes toys, digital devices, rocks, trees, animals, people, all that is nature, and the universe as a whole. This is why you are never really alone when you live through the *peaceful light of your core-Self* in *the timeless moment of Now.*

Precious One, when you hug someone you love, you feel a close oneness with them inside your heart and your whole body. This close oneness you feel when you are hugging somebody you love is not just a close oneness that only happens with people. You can also feel a caring oneness and a heartfelt closeness with all beings and things through the peaceful light of your core-Self in *the timeless moment of Now*

Precious One, when you feel a tender closeness and a caring oneness with any being or thing in your everyday life, you are really feeling *a timeless moment of love* with the whole universe. This *timeless moment of love* with the whole universe happens when you lovingly take care of each being and thing from the peaceful light of your core-Self. As you live just like this, you are really being the body of love while endlessly sharing love in the *peaceful light of Now.*

Being Her Still Peaceful Light,
She Enjoys Core-Self Friendship
With All Beings And Things

How You Forget Your Peaceful Light

Precious One, from the time you were born, your core-Self has been your true-Self that has no name. When you were a baby, you did not know anything about letters, words, or numbers. You did not know about your brain or your personal self with a name. You did not know that your personal name would begin to live inside your brain. Still, you were happy just being the peaceful light of your core-Self that always felt like a warm glowing stillness at the center of your body.

Precious One, right after you were born, your mom and dad gave you a special name. This was your birth name that others would call you for the rest of your life. You did not know that you would be a self with a name that lives inside your brain. You did not know that you would be daily thinking and talking about your *I, me, and mine.*

Precious One, when you were being cared for as a baby, your mom and dad always called you by your name. This is how you began to know that you are a separate self with a name. As you learned to speak with words, you started to talk and play with others who also called you by your name. This is why your personal self with a name became who you think you are inside your brain.

Precious One, you first learned how to talk and think with words at home. Then you went to school with other children. At school and with your friends, you began to learn how to read words, understand numbers, and use laptops and other digital devices to learn many things. All this is how your personal self with a name began to feel like a very smart thinking brain. As your personal self with a name felt more like a smart thinking brain, you lost touch with the warm still glow of your core-Self at the center of your whole body. This is how you forgot about the great smartness of a peaceful light that you share with all beings and things in *the timeless moment of Now.*

She Knows How To Rest All
Her Thinking And Learning In
The Peaceful Light Of Her Core-Self.

The Personal Self Inside Your Brain

Precious One, your personal self with a name that lives inside your brain is not the true-Self you felt as a baby. The true-Self that you felt as a baby is your core-Self that has no name. This does not mean that your personal self is not real. Your personal self with a name that lives inside your brain is very real and important.

Precious One, your personal self can think, know, and speak about many things. Your personal self tries to take care of people and fix things through the growing smartness of the brain. Your personal self with a name helps you remember that you are part of a very special family with all its relatives and ancestors.

Precious One, as you grow older, you will see how important it is to have a personal self that others can trust and respect.

People want to know that they can depend on your personal self to fulfill responsibilities and keep promises. People want to know that your personal self is being sincere, honest, and truthful when sharing facts, feelings, ideas, and memories.

Precious One, your personal self uses thinking to understand all the passing thoughts, sensations, and feelings that are happening inside your body. Your personal self also uses thinking to understand all the people, things, and events that you meet in your daily life. There will be times when all this thinking will make you feel stressed, upset, and anxious. At other times, you will feel helpless and frustrated because you can't stop all the thoughts and thinking that just keep happening inside your brain. This is why it is so important to sit quietly alone each day, breathe into your body core center, and feel the warm still glow of your peaceful light. Then the peaceful light of your core-Self will bring an easeful gladness to your distressed heart and a still calmness to your overworked brain.

*Feeling The Still Warm Glow Of
Core-Self, Their Hearts And Minds
Are Peacefully Clear And Bright.*

People Who Sleep In Their Thinking Brain

Precious One, when you sit quietly alone each day and breathe into the warm still glow of your core-Self, you will experience the *great smartness of your peaceful light* that connects you to all beings and things. Then your whole body will feel totally alert and awake in *the timeless moment of Now* that happens everywhere all at once.

Precious One, when people do not take time to daily experience the warm still glow of their core-Self, they will easily fall asleep in their personal self with a name and their thinking brain. This means that they fall fast asleep in all their figuring and thinking, all their judging and believing, and all their thoughts about *I, me, and mine.* If people remain fast asleep in their heads just like this, they will not wake up to the *peaceful light of their core-Self* nor experience the *timeless moment of Now* that connects them to all beings and things.

Precious One, when people fall fast asleep in their self with a name and their thinking brain, they feel that something important is missing that they really need. They think that they will feel happier and more alive when they finally find what's missing and get what they need. This is why they keep searching for things they can own or possess; things that excite or relax their bodies; things that numb their hearts or drug their minds; things that stimulate or depress their brains; things that make them feel famous or powerful; and things to believe in that make them feel right without ever being wrong.

Precious One, instead of finding what they really need, people only find an unsteady happiness that comes and goes. They do not know that what they need has always been at the center of their whole body. They do not know that they can be a glowing aliveness and a steady happiness just as they are. All they have to do is sit quietly alone each day, breathe into their body center, and feel *the warm still glow of their peaceful light.* Then they will wake up from all their sleeping and stop all their seeking. Then they will daily enjoy *the great smartness of their core-Self in the timeless moment of Now.*

Asleep In His Thinking Brain,
He Does Not Feel The Peaceful
Light At The Center Of His Body.

Stay Awake To The Peaceful Light Of Now

Precious One, some people who are fast asleep in their thinking brain want to be with people who look like them and think like them. Others may feel superior to anyone who has a different color skin. They don't like to be with people who talk, pray, or live differently than they do. If you meet people like this, they may say mean and hateful things about your race, your sexual orientation, or your personal beliefs. If you are not awake to who you really are as core-Self inside your body, you will feel abused, deeply hurt, and very angry. Then you will do or say something to get back at them. You may even build a wall around your tender heart and hide the special nature of your personal self from the judgement of others.

Precious One, if you keep distancing people from your tender heart and hiding the special nature of your personal self from the judgement of others, you will begin to feel unhappy, cranky, stressed, and lonely. Sometimes you might feel scared, irritated, and mad. You might feel so much hurt, stress, and anger inside your body that you will be grouchy and unloving all day long. All this will not make you feel happier or healthier. It will only make you feel sadder, worn-out, upset, and more likely to get sick.

Precious One, when you are feeling hurt, stressed, and angry, just breathe into the center of your body. Then you will start to feel the warm still glow of your core-Self. As you experience your core-Self, your whole body will enjoy *the peaceful light of Now.* Then you will remember who you really are before your personal self, your race, your sexual orientation, and all your beliefs. The *peaceful light of Now* will start to heal your hurt, anger, sadness, and loneliness. Then the walls around your heart will begin to melt away. Your thinking brain will feel sharper and clearer. You will feel more confident, alert, and at ease in your body. Then you will gladly share the special nature of your personal self with all its thoughts and feelings. This is how you can be a happier, healthier, and more loving human being.

Sad, Hurt, And Lonely, He
Breathes Into His Center To Feel
The Healing Light Of His Core-Self.

Meet Life Challenges From Your Peaceful Light

Precious One, when people are wide awake to the warm still glow of their core-Self, they trust the great smartness of its peaceful light that guides them in everyday life. Of course, this does not mean that they do not use the smartness of their brain or the smartness of their heart. They absolutely do. However, they rely on the great smartness of core-Self to peacefully guide their daily thinking and all their passing feelings while living, loving, working, playing, and being.

Precious One, in our daily life, we all go through hardships, challenges and difficult emotions. Many of these distressing events and emotions cannot be understood, fixed, or healed by the smartness of our heart or the smartness of our brain. People all feel a deep sadness, helplessness, and confusion when someone they love dies. Some of us may get a life threatening illness or have a serious injury that needs surgery. Some people may be bullied so much that they are constantly fearful, timid, and stressed-out. Others feel judged, unaccepted, and isolated, because they are different and don't fit in. These and many other distressing events and emotions can become a part of peoples lives.

Precious One, as you live through your own life challenges, do not try to fix your problems or heal your distressing emotions with just your heart or your brain. If you do, you may begin to feel more frustrated, angry, and confused. You may even begin to think that there is nothing you can do to solve your problems or heal your difficult emotions. All this happens when you only rely on the smartness of your brain and the smartness of your heart.

Precious One, if you stay awake to the warm still glow of your core-Self, you will know with your whole body that the great smartness of your peaceful light can totally assist the smartness of your heart and the smartness of your brain. Then you will courageously and confidently pass through challenging events, stressful hardships, and difficult emotions while being core-Self in *the peaceful light of Now.*

A Smiling Gorilla Points To The
Great Smartness Of Her Peaceful
Light That Guides Her Way Every Day.

Wake Up To Your Peaceful Light Every Morning

Precious One, the peaceful light of your core-Self is always ready to guide you from the time you open your eyes in the morning until you close them at night. This is why I encourage you to greet the peaceful light of your core-Self before you get out of bed.

Precious One, when you first wake up in bed, keep lying on your back. Then gently close your eyes and start to breathe only through your nose. Follow each in-breath into your body center just below your belly button. There you will begin to feel the warm still glow of your core-Self. After five in-breaths, gently open your eyes, do a whole body stretch, and then sit up to get out of bed.

Precious One, after you get out of bed, go to the bathroom, splash water on your face, brush your teeth, get dressed, and comb your hair. Once you are dressed, clean, and wide awake, sit down alone for five minutes. You can sit on a chair or on the floor with a pillow. Keep your eyes half-open and breathe gently through your nose. Remember to follow each in-breath into your body core-Self center. After five minutes, put your palms together near your heart and bow a little from your waist. Then you can slowly get up and start doing the things you need to do from the peaceful light of your core-Self.

Precious One, if the self with a name inside your brain begins to complain about the things you need to get done, do not moan or groan. Do not feel sorry for yourself or whine and grumble to others. Do not fall fast asleep in your *I, me, and mine.* Just breathe into your body center and feel the warm still glow of your core-Self. Then, if things need to get done, just do them in *the timeless moment of Now.* Do them with an open heart from the great smartness of your peaceful light. When you do things just like this, all your grumbling and groaning will fade away. All your moaning and whining will simply stop. Then you will know that whatever you get done through the peaceful light of your core-Self will make the world a better place for you and all beings and things.

A Tiger Wakes Up Each Morning
To Meet The Jungle From The Great
Smartness Of His Peaceful Light.

Trust The Peaceful Light To Unfold Your Future

Precious One, each morning, as you greet the peaceful light of your core-Self, it will faithfully guide all your thinking, feeling, loving, and living. The great smartness of your peaceful light will show you what is true and not true, what is good and not good, what is love and not love, and what is healthy and not healthy. This is why I encourage you to fully trust the felt guidance of your peaceful light during each day. When you do just this, the peaceful light of your core-Self unfolds an ever surprising and fulfilling future just for you.

Precious One, as you trust the felt guidance of your peaceful light to unfold your ever surprising and fulfilling future, thoughts of worry and doubt may begin to pass through your thinking brain. If these thoughts of worry and doubt begin to stress and overwhelm the self with a name inside your brain, just breathe

27

into your center and feel the warm still glow of your peaceful light. Then all your passing thoughts of worry and doubt will melt away. Then your self with a name will rest at ease inside your brain. This is how you will recover the calmness, courage, and confidence to live from the felt guidance of your peaceful light. Then you will feel totally reassured that the peaceful light of your core-Self is unfolding your ever surprising and fulfilling future in *the timeless moment of Now*

Precious One, all this does not mean that you should not use your thinking brain. You can absolutely use your thinking brain to set personal goals and envision a successful future for yourself. However, as you use your thinking brain to envision your future, stay in touch with the felt guidance of your peaceful light. Then your peaceful light will always remind you that loving yourself, while joyfully loving and serving others, is the most fulfilling and successful future that you can start living right here and now.

Palms Together In Deep Gratitude,
He Entrusts The Unfolding Of His Future
To The Felt Guidance Of His Peaceful Light.

Accept Your Whole Life And All Your Feelings

Precious One, as you daily live from the felt guidance of your peaceful light, you will learn to accept your life just as it is. When you accept your life just as it is, you will feel the great smartness of the whole universe right where you are. As you feel the great smartness of the whole universe right where you are, you will accept each moment of your life with the fearless courage and still calmness of your core-Self.

Precious One, accepting your life just as it is does not mean that you have to like each moment that is happening. You can certainly dislike what's happening, but disliking it while grumbling and complaining to yourself and others does not change it. It is better to breathe into your body center, feel the warm still glow of your core-Self, and tenderly accept what's happening through your peaceful light. Once you accept whats happening without trying to push it away, your core-Self will guide you to courageously grow as a loving and caring human being through the happening itself.

29

Precious One, as you accept your life just as it is, you will also learn to accept all your feelings just as they are. It does not matter whether you feel happy or sad, hurt or angry. It does not matter whether you are feeling pain or pleasure. When you accept all your feelings through the peaceful light of your core-Self, you will know that each feeling is really the great smartness of the whole universe. Once you understand this, you will naturally want to learn from all the feelings you have inside your body.

Precious One, when you accept each passing moment of your life and all your arising feelings, you will live with a peaceful mind and a grateful heart. You will experience the great smartness of the whole universe in everything you feel and do. Your body will be a deep joy and happiness whether you are alone or with others. Then you will always treasure the peaceful light of your core-Self that helps you accept your whole life and all your feelings just as they are.

When All Human Beings Know That
Their Feelings Are The Same, They Will
Accept Each Other Just As They Are.

Accept Death And Dying Just As They Are

Precious One, when you accept life just as it is, you will be curious about death and dying. You will want to know what happens when people die. At first, you may find an answer in your family's religion. You may even read about other religions around the world. However, any religion will give your thinking brain an answer that cannot be proven. When you want to accept a religious answer that cannot be proven, your thinking brain will make a mental leap of faith that needs no proof. Then you will study and practice your religious answer with others who believe like you. This is how you will learn to live and die with faith in the religious answer you have found.

Precious One, whether you believe in a religious answer or not, I encourage you to experience the felt answer of your core-Self that is softly whispered at the center of your body. All you have to do is sit quietly alone, breathe into your core-Self center, and feel the warm still glow of your peaceful light. When you do just this, the still glow of your peaceful light will prove to your whole body that the One great smartness of the infinite universe exists in both life and death. Then your whole body will be at peace with death and dying just as they are.

Precious One, when you feel at peace with death and dying, you will realize that your whole body is experiencing and being faith without the support of any religious belief. Then you will understand that a mental leap of faith into believing is not the same as the whole body confidently being faith without beliefs or believing.

Precious One, once your whole body is being faith in *the timeless moment of Now,* you will cherish the One great smartness of life and death that no religious belief can ever own or fully understand. As you cherish the One great smartness of life and death, your peaceful light will daily guide you to live truthfully, care tenderly, and love faithfully during the passage of time. So while you are alive, trust the felt guidance of your peaceful light, live from your whole body of faith, and meet death and dying just as they are.

*Trusting The Still Glow Of His
Peaceful Light, He Simply Accepts
Death And Dying Just As They Are.*

The Awesome Hug Of A Whole Universe

Precious One, when you accept your whole life, all your passing feelings, and death and dying just as they are, you will daily feel an awesome hug inside your body. This awesome hug is from the One great smartness of the whole universe that happens in both life and death.

Precious One, the awesome hug of the whole universe is really a warm feeling of peace and well-being that starts happening at your core center and spreads everywhere inside your body. When you feel this peace and well-being throughout your body, you will know that you are being hugged by the One great smartness of the whole universe in *the timeless moment of Now.*

Precious One, as you live with the awesome hug of the whole universe inside your body, you will understand that all human beings are being hugged as brothers and sisters just as they are. It does not matter their age, the color of their skin, the language they speak, how intelligent they are, what they believe in, how much money they make, or the country of their birth. All human beings are being hugged together as a worldwide family by the One great smartness of the whole universe in *the peaceful light of Now.* This truth is softly whispered at the core-Self center of all human beings from the time of their birth until the time of their death and dying.

Precious One, all people can feel the awesome hug of the whole universe inside their body. It does not matter how old or young they are. All they have to do is sit quietly alone each day, breathe into their center, and feel the warm still glow of their core-Self. Then they will stop sleeping in their thinking brain, their self with a name, their different beliefs, and all their thoughts about I, me, and mine. Then they will wake up to the felt guidance of their peaceful light, enjoy the awesome hug of the whole universe together, and treat each other as just one family in *the timeless moment of Now.*

He Dances With Joy As
He Feels The Awesome Hug
Of The Whole Universe.

A Future World Of Peaceful Light

Precious One, there will be a time when all people will live from the peaceful light of their core-Self while enjoying the awesome hug of the whole universe. This will be a time when all human beings will live together as just one family of caring brothers and sisters. Then people will treat each other with mutual respect, speak to each other truthfully, think together honestly, and listen to each other with a sincere and open heart.

Precious One, I want you to know that all this will happen in a future world filled with peaceful light. I want you to imagine this future world before you sit quietly alone to meet the warm still glow of your core-Self. Imagine a world without racial prejudice, hateful speech, social injustice, sexual inequality, and global terrorism. Imagine all nations taking good care of people's health, safety, and education. Imagine all countries protecting our planet's well-being and nature's delicate balance. Imagine world leaders safeguarding the freedoms of speech, thought, sexual identity, and religious belief. Imagine a world where warfare no longer exists. Imagine a world where all people stay awake to the great smartness of their core-Self in *the timeless moment of Now.* Then imagine all religions being guided by the peaceful light at the core-Self center of all human beings.

Precious One, as you sit quietly alone breathing into your core-Self center, I want you to know that this future world is not a daydream or a made-up fantasy inside your brain. This future world is daily felt by the still calmness of your core-Self and foreseen by the inner vision of your peaceful light. All people from the time of their birth until the time of their death are called by core-Self to faithfully create this future world through the still smart center of their whole body.

Precious One, this future world may seem far away in time, but it is always ready to be lived for yourself and others right where you are. Just be the peaceful light of core-Self during the passage of everyday time. Then you will know that this future world is always being born through what you say and do. So continue to treat all human beings with equality and respect, trust the felt guidance of your peaceful light, take good care of your whole life and all your feelings, and enjoy the awesome hug of the whole universe inside your body.

Smiling From Ear To Ear,
A Frog Waves From A Future
World Filled With Peaceful Light.

Many People Think We Are Foolish Dreamers,
But We Are Really Awake To Our Inner Sight.
When Human Beings Live As Just One Family,
Our Whole World Will Glow In Peaceful Light.

Breathing Into The Core-Self Center Of Our Body,
We Accept Our Whole Life And All Our Feelings,
Being The Still Warm Glow Of Our Peaceful Light,
We Enjoy The Awesome Hug Of The Whole Universe.